Did you know?

The motto of the Olympic Games is "Faster, Higher, Stronger!"

Have you ever seen the Olympics?

The world's top **athletes** take part in the Games. They all want to win a gold medal.

The first Games

The Olympic Games were first held in Greece about 3000 years ago.

Contents

C0055 71983

Sounds in this book

a (want)   ear (years) eer (cheers)
e-e (athletes)   ir (first) o (host)   old (gold)
or (work)   sion (television)   ture (future)

A festival of sport

The Olympic Games are a fantastic festival of sport. They take place every four years.

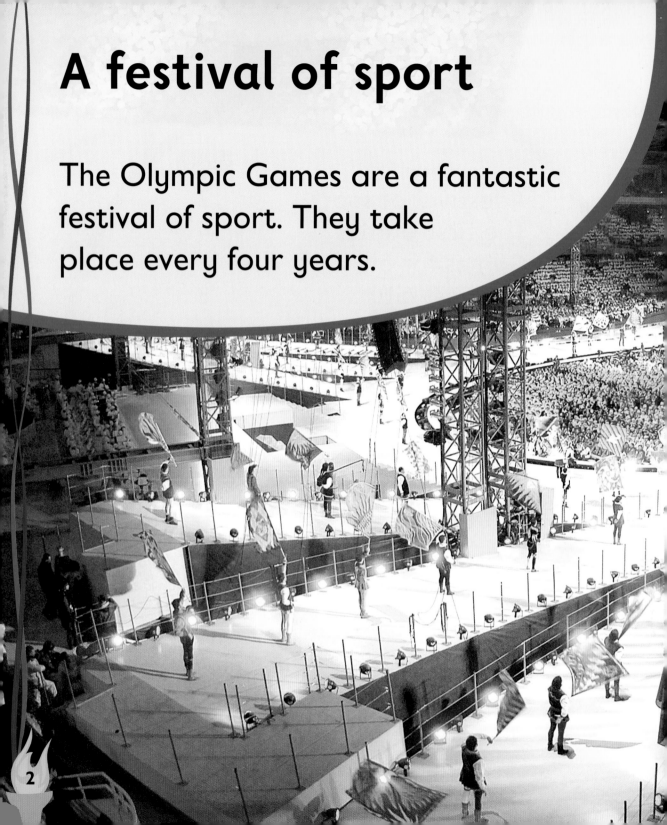

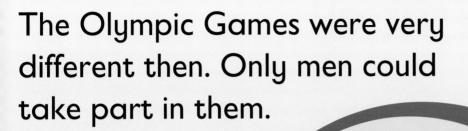

The Olympic Games were very different then. Only men could take part in them.

There are athletes on this Greek pot.

Did you know?

There were no medals in the old Games. Instead, winners got a crown of leaves.

5

Games for all

Today there are three sets of Olympic Games. One set is held in the summer. Another set takes place in the winter.

Sailing in the summer

Skiing in the winter

Athletes at the Paralympics

There are Olympic Games for athletes with disabilities, too. They are called the **Paralympics**.

The host city

Lots of cities in the world want to **host** the Olympic Games. London has been chosen to host the Games in 2012.

This is the site for the London Olympics.

To host the Olympics, a city needs
lots of things, including:

- a site for the sports to take place
- a swimming pool
- places for all the athletes to stay.

About 10,000 athletes take part in the summer Olympic Games!

Training for the Games

Every athlete dreams of being in the Olympic Games. They train to be as good as they can.

Training is very hard work!

The British team arrives at the 2008 Olympic Games.

If they are lucky and work very hard, athletes may be chosen to join the Olympic team.

The Olympic torch

The Olympic torch is lit for every Olympic games. It is lit in Greece, and then it is taken to the host city.

The torch has a long trip to the Olympic games.

Did you know?

In 2008, the Olympic torch took 130 days to get from Greece to China.

When the torch gets there, it is time for the Games to begin!

The Games open

At the start of the Olympic Games, there is music and fireworks.

Did you know?

Teams come from all over the world.

These athletes belong to the team from Canada.

The crowd cheers athletes from each country.

A fortnight of sport

The Olympic Games last for a fortnight. All over the world people watch the Games on television and the Internet.

Cameras record an Olympic event for TV, newspapers and the Internet.

Winning a medal

The top three athletes in each sport win a medal.

Who has won the gold medal?

The athlete in third place wins a bronze medal. The athlete in second place wins a silver medal. The winning athlete gets a gold medal.

Did you know?

The youngest person ever to win a medal was a 10-year-old boy! He took part in the Olympic Games in 1896.

The Games close

When the Games are over,
the Olympic torch is put out.

The end of the
Olympic Games.

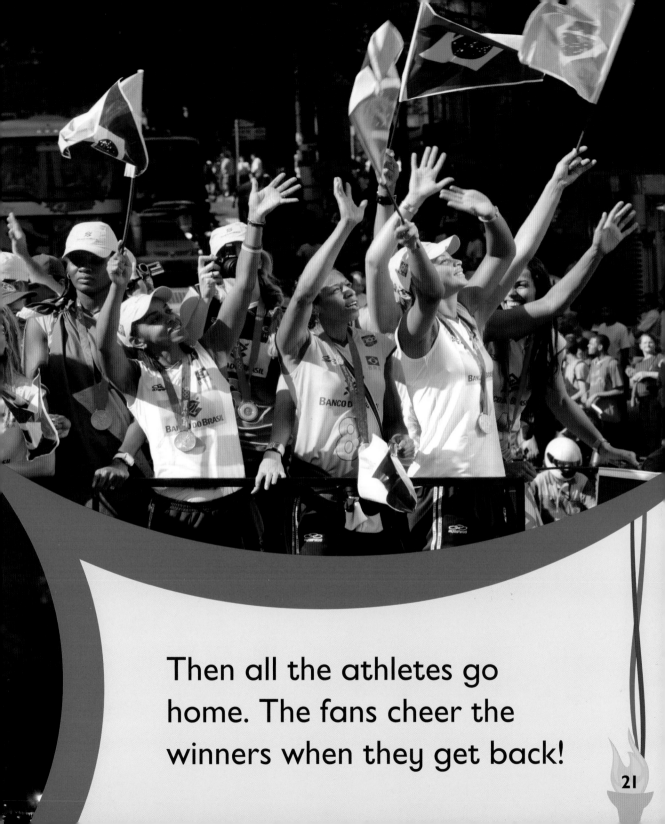

Then all the athletes go home. The fans cheer the winners when they get back!

A future star?

All over the world, athletes are training hard for the next Olympic Games.

Young athletes training

Do you enjoy sport? Could you train to be the best? Perhaps, one day, you will take part in the Olympic Games!

Running is fun! Which sport do **you** like best?

Glossary

Athlete: a sportsperson who takes part in a race or sporting event

Host: the host city is the city where the Olympic Games takes place

Paralympics: the Olympic Games for athletes with disabilities

Index